£1·62

Proficiency English

10
81

Also by W.S. Fowler

Proficiency English Book 1: Language and Composition
Proficiency English Book 2: Reading Comprehension
Proficiency English Book 4: Listening Comprehension
First Certificate English Books 1—4
Dictionary of Idioms

with John Pidcock and Robin Rycroft

First Certificate English Book 5
Incentive English, an international course
Proficiency English Book 5: Interview

with Norman Coe

Nelson English Language Tests Books 1—3
Test Your English Books 1 and 2
Quickcheck Tests

Proficiency English

Book 3: Use of English

Teacher's Guide

W.S. Fowler

Nelson

Thomas Nelson and Sons Ltd
Nelson House   Mayfield Road
Walton-on-Thames   Surrey KT12 5PL
P O Box 18123   Nairobi   Kenya
Watson Estate   Block A   13 Floor
Watson Road   Causeway Bay   Hong Kong
116-D JTC Factory Building
Lorong 3   Geylang Square   Singapore 14

Thomas Nelson Australia Pty Ltd
19-39 Jeffcott Street   West Melbourne   Victoria 3003

Nelson Canada Ltd
81 Curlew Drive   Don Mills   Ontario M3A 2R1

Thomas Nelson (Nigeria) Ltd
8 Ilupeju Bypass   PMB21303   Ikeja   Lagos

First published 1978
Reprinted 1979, 1980
ISBN 0 17 555144 8
NCN 8633-71-2

Printed in Hong Kong

Contents

Introduction

General Points on Presentation

The Use of English, for the reasons outlined in the Introduction to the Student's Book, can easily become little more than a guessing game in the classroom situation. What is most valuable to the student, both from the point of view of the Cambridge Proficiency examination and in terms of developing skills which will be of use to him outside the classroom, is that he should be able to recognise modern English usage. This should be seen as a necessary stage towards his being able to use the language himself in a variety of circumstances.

Proficiency English Book 3 is meant to be used throughout a course beginning immediately after students have passed, or reached a level equivalent to, Cambridge First Certificate. Ideally, it should be used in conjunction with the other books in the *Proficiency English* course, and teachers will find it helpful to look at the Table on p. 14, indicating the way in which Use of English lessons can fit into an overall teaching plan.

Section One – English in Use

The passages chosen for this section have been graded in order of increasing difficulty so that two could be done each term in a two-year course. The lessons are based on the form of the Use of English paper (Section B), but also provide questions of the type used in Section A, and give practice in summary. Students should be methodically trained in this skill, and I believe that the technique demonstrated in Lesson 1 is the most practical for the purpose.

I would like to emphasise that the exercises here should not be done as tests. They are an opportunity for students to develop their awareness of the language together. Students should therefore be encouraged to offer alternatives to the first correct answer given, because in many cases there are a number of ways of saying the same thing in English. The real value of such practice lies much deeper, since what indicates fluency in a speaker of English is very often the fact that he is capable of paraphrasing what he hears – in other words, saying the same thing in a different way. This, in turn, is a necessary stage towards being able to rephrase something said in one's own words, giving it one's own characteristic style. It is obvious that in the context of the examination this is valuable for summary and for the kind of exercise presented in Section Two of this book, but in the wider context of real life it is of great importance for anyone who must convey the main points of what he has heard (at a conference or business meeting, for example) to someone else. My recommendation, therefore, is that once the passage has been read and discussed – and there is no reason why the subject of the passage should not be used for discussion, just because 'this is a Use of English lesson' – students should be put into small groups of three or four to work on the questions. In this way, more possible alternatives will be offered to the teacher for comment, and everyone will become more familiar with the problems and techniques of rephrasing.

Some attempts at rephrasing are likely to lead to disagreement as to whether an answer is acceptable. In the answers, I have tried to put forward alternatives which I think are instantly acceptable to a native English speaker. I may have left out some highly ingenious para-phrases, and here the teacher must rely on his own ear and experi-ence. But it is far more likely that he will be offered not the kind of paraphrase that would occur to a native English speaker, but some-thing that is really a half-translation from the student's own language. Once again, in dealing with such queries, the teacher should remember that these exercises are not tests where half-marks are awarded for something approximating to English speech and writing. What matters to the student in this situation is that he should learn to recognise what we say, not find some grammatically correct, un-English alternative to what we say. Therefore, if a student is asked to paraphrase:

Perhaps she missed her train
I would expect the answer
She may (or *she might*) *have missed her train*
but it would be misleading to the student to allow
It is possible that she (has) missed her train
without commenting that it is not the most natural way of saying it.
I would comment in the same way on
Possibly, she missed her train
and would not accept
She possibly missed her train
under any circumstances.

In general, these problems are overcome by the pointers given to the conversion – either 'She may . . .' or MAY in this case – but there is no harm in them occurring, even though the teacher's explanation may be no more than: 'I'm sorry. There's nothing wrong with it gram-matically but we just don't say that.'

Section Two – Using English in Different Circumstances

Here I have tried to cover the wide range of topics possible in Section B, question 2, of the Cambridge Proficiency examination, which varies from year to year. Teachers using the book in conjunction with *Book 1: Language and Composition* will recognise the connection between this kind of exercise and the passages in Section Three of that book,

Types of Modern English. The difference is one of emphasis, since in all cases here the student is being asked to imitate appropriate styles of writing in different circumstances, as well as being trained to recognise the kind of language employed. The teaching technique to be adopted should be one of drawing attention to the stylistic norms presented. For a more detailed consideration of these styles, see the Notes on pp. 12–13.

Section Three – Progress Tests

This series of progress papers will prove more difficult for students who are not using Book 1 of the course, though it represents a valid testing medium in its own right. The reason for this is that in each paper I have concentrated heavily on the structures presented in that book. If used in conjunction with Book 1, the progress papers should be given as follows:

1 after Lesson 2 *(Proficiency English 1)*; 2 after Lesson 4; 3 after Lesson 6; 4 after Lesson 8; 5 after Lesson 11; 6 after Lesson 15. Once again the Table on p. 14 will be of help in planning classes. In this connection, but also in connection with the Selective Cloze Tests at the end of each lesson in Section One, students may be tempted to refer back to the original in order to 'get it right'. Obviously, this is counter-productive, and if the teacher emphasises from the outset that the student who does this loses the opportunity of developing his powers of recognition, it is to be hoped that students will be intelligent enough not to misuse the book. It is true that memory, as well as recognition, may play a part, which is why the Selective Cloze Tests in Section One are always placed at the end of the lesson, but I must again insist that even the progress papers are only tests in the diagnostic sense that they give the teacher an indication of what needs to be revised. The index at the back of this Guide, referring to the structures presented in Book 1, will be helpful to teachers using the two books together. The progress papers can be attempted as tests or as group work on the lines indicated above for Section One. If you use all or part of the tests under exam conditions, award one mark for each correct answer. The pass mark should be 60–65%.

Section Four – Test Papers

This section summarises everything taught in the previous sections, providing Test Papers to be attempted in the final stage before taking the examination. The tests are of the same format and length as the examination itself. Three hours should be allowed for completion, or, alternatively, one hour for Section A and one hour each for the different parts of Section B.

If you set all or part of the Test Papers under exam conditions, award 50 marks for Section A (one mark per question), 30 for question 5 (15 for the summary), and 20 for question 6.

Will Fowler, Barcelona, June 1977

Notes on the Different Sections of the Book

Section One – English in Use

The only additional notes of value here are items of cultural information which should be given to students before or during their reading of the text.

1 A Space in the Country

rec (1.5). Recreation ground. The difference between this and a park should be defined.

Government White Paper (1.8). Report placed before Parliament, usually as a preliminary stage to proposals embodied in a Bill.

The Countryside Commission (ll.40–1) is a Government body, while the *National Trust* (1.43) is private. Both are concerned with conserving and improving the environment.

3 Showing the Flag

Princess Elizabeth Day Committee (1.14). The Princess is now Queen Elizabeth II.

Queen Alexandra (1.16). Wife of Edward VII, King from 1901 to 1910.

Gainsborough hats (1.27). Large, floppy, flowered hats, so called because they are worn by many ladies in the portraits of the eighteenth-century painter Thomas Gainsborough.

Prince of Wales's National Relief Fund (1.33). At that time, the Prince of Wales was Edward, later King Edward VIII (1936).

Pontypool (1.39). A town in Monmouthshire, South Wales.

The Belgians (1.58). The reason for this collection was that Belgium was the first country invaded by Germany in 1914.

Oxfam (1.63). An organisation devoted to working for charity.

4 Economy Drive

£1 gallon forecast (ll.3–4). A gallon is about 4.5 litres.

Lord Stokes (1.4). Then Chairman and Managing Director of British Leyland, the largest British-owned car manufacturer.

90 mph (1.20). 90 miles per hour, or about 144 kilometres per hour.

mpg (1.39). Miles per gallon.

Brands Hatch (1.42). A motor racing circuit in Kent.

8 Liberty v. Equality

The Scottish educational system is independent of that of England and Wales. Hence, it has developed differently. The author of this article is a Labour MP, so his approach to the problem of parental choice for schools and interpretation of parental freedom is different from that of Conservatives.

10 Greenwich Newly Observed

Greenwich (l.1). A suburb south of the River Thames, down river from the City of London.
Cutty Sark (l.3). A nineteenth-century ship.
Islington and Hampstead (l.21). Suburbs in the north of London, fashionable in recent years among young professional people.
King's Road, Chelsea (ll.27–8). The centre of the boutique business in London.
DoE (l.40). Department of the Environment.
Georgian (l.41). Of the reign of George IV (1820–30).
GLC (l.47). Greater London Council.
Tower, Charing Cross (l.51). River stations on the Thames, in this context. The Tower is of course the Tower of London, Charing Cross a railway station.

12 The Sun Sinks Slowly on the Western

The Duke (ll.7–8). Nickname given to John Wayne.
prime-time (l.14). An American expression, meaning the time of day when television attracts its largest audiences.
High Noon (l.31). Made in 1952 by Fred Zinnemann, starring Gary Cooper.
The Wild Bunch (l.32). Made in 1968 by Sam Peckinpah, starring William Holden.

Section Two – Using English in Special Circumstances

Letters to the Editor

The style of these letters is typical of those that appear in 'quality' newspapers. Note the use of cliché – 'the powers that be', 'the natural order of things', 'I have no axe to grind' – in the first letter. While the second letter has its share of cliché – the use of the word 'chauvinistic', for example – it is a much better model for students, who are likely to be in trouble if they try to reproduce cliché and do not, in any case, benefit from doing so. The style of the first might well be, judging from past experience, the one used in the examination itself as an example, but students would normally be expected to reply to it in their own words.

Offa's Dyke (first correspondent's address) was built by the Mercian king Offa in the 8th century to divide his Saxon kingdom from Wales! *Cymru* (third correspondent's address) is of course Wales in Welsh.

Speeches

Again, the kind of speech students would be expected to write is much more likely to resemble the second example, though the first contains useful pointers towards the style of informal speeches (see q. 1, 4 and 5). I have deliberately avoided the extremes of jocular cliché common on occasions like that of the first speech.

Telegrams and News Reports

These are not so much an examination topic as an encouragement to group work. (See *Proficiency English Book 1, TG*, p. 24, where I suggest that this kind of practice can easily be developed, using any recent English newspaper, as an aid to paragraph writing.)

The examples I have given are also useful for vocabulary development, since they reflect the vocabulary of headlines and sub-heads in newspapers without employing the more extreme, totally incomprehensible (for a foreigner) puns frequently used in banner headlines.

Recommendations, Schedules, Regulations

Here, the main point from a stylistic point of view is emphasised in the Student's Book. Students are unlikely to be surprised by the use of 'should' for recommendations, or 'will' for a statement of events that are going to take place. The use of 'shall' in Example C can be justified by the need to make what is said legally binding. Compare: *They will come* or *They won't come* (statement of fact or intention) with *They shall come* (I insist on it) or *They shan't come* (I'll prevent it).

Reviewing

This is unlikely to be the kind of question set in Section B of the Proficiency Use of English paper. However, it is good training in writing English in a style which either praises something without being gushing or vague, or else criticises it without being unpleasantly aggressive. The exercises give students the opportunity to attack or defend something in appropriate language, an exercise which can obviously be extended to a wide range of other subjects.

Hitchcockian (second paragraph): in the style of Alfred Hitchcock, the great Anglo-American film director

Kafkaesque (second paragraph): mysteriously claustrophobic, in the style of the writer Franz Kafka

Propaganda

The value of this, apart from demonstrating the techniques of repetition and the use of slogans common to persuasive language of all kinds, is really to be seen in conjunction with the Dialogue. It is worth asking students to look at the way in which the same information is conveyed in more colloquial language in the Dialogue.

Suggested Work Plan

Teachers using this book in conjunction with other books in the *Proficiency English* series may find this table helpful in planning lessons, though it is by no means intended to be a rigidly schematic approach. At the same time, I am convinced that all the different kinds of practice included in the course should be used together, instead of the books being taught consecutively, partly because it provides classes with greater variety and partly because the skills are in many cases interdependent.

The suggested plan below presupposes six terms or working periods.

Term	Book 1	Book 2	Book 3
1	Section 1(1–4)	Lessons 1–4 Lexical Test 1	Section 1(1–2) Section 3(1–2)
2	Section 1(5–6) Start Sections 2A, 2B and 3	Lessons 5–8 Lexical Test 2	Section 1(3–4) Section 3(3)
3	Section 1(7–8) Finish Sections 2A, 2B and 3	Lessons 9–12 Lexical Test 3	Section 1(5–6) Section 3(4)
4	Section 1(9–11) Section 2C	Lessons 13–16 Lexical Test 4	Section 1(7–8) Section 3(5)
5	Section 1(12–15) Begin Section 4	Lessons 17–20 Lexical Test 5	Section 1(9–10) Begin Section 2 Section 3(6)
6	Finish Section 4	Lessons 21–24 Lexical Test 6 Test Papers	Section 1(11–12) Finish Section 2 Section 4

Answers

Section One: English in Use

Lesson 1 A Space in the Country

C

1 It has been carried out so quietly that many people are unaware of what has been achieved (*or* It has been so quietly carried out . . .).
2 People settle down somewhere in the country, making life inconvenient and expensive for the countryman (*or* making the countryman's life inconvenient . . .).
3 They all have car parks.
4 You may have to pay an admission fee (*or* you may be charged . . .).
5 An admission fee may be charged.
6 The Countryside Commission carried out a survey showing (*or* which/that showed) that over 200,000 people visited the parks.

D

1 Many people do not know what has been achieved.
2 Ten years ago the country park was only an idea.
3 They settle down where they feel like it (*or* feel comfortable, at ease, etc.).
4 A good country park will be within easy reach.
5 A good country park will be readily accessible by car and on foot.

E

1 place
2 so
3 it
4 out (through)
5 little
6 what
7 Don't (Never)
8 or
9 as
10 two (alternatives)
11 on
12 than
13 ago (back)
14 nothing (little) (hardly)
15 an
16 called (entitled) (headed)
17 there
18 over
19 every
20 in

Lesson 2 How Safe are British Dams?

C

1 Events such as (like) these raise again the question of dam safety in Britain.
2 In Britain, age is the element that seems to pose the most risk (*or* age seems to be the element that poses . . .).
3 There is no such thing as perfect legislation.
4 Authorities have rarely been prosecuted for failing (failure) to remedy a defective dam.
5 Some dams have never been inspected although there is a statutory obligation to do so (*or* a statutory obligation to do so exists).

D

1 Two dams in Brazil collapsed as a result of weeks of torrential rain (*or* As a result of weeks of torrential . . . collapsed) (*or* The result of weeks of torrential rain in Brazil was that two dams collapsed).
2 Such events bring up again the question of dam safety in Britain.
3 The Reservoirs Act, 1975, is still to be put into effect.
4 Most dam failures take place soon after construction or after a long uneventful period of operation.
5 The new Act makes 66 local authorities responsible for enforcement of its legislation (*or* 66 local authorities have been made responsible . . . by the new Act).
6 Local authorities do not always carry out (through) the dictates of Parliament.

E

withstand (resist); doubtless (probably); demand, require; eventually, finally; indicated.

F

1 tend	11 owe
2 or	12 Until
3 appears (seems)	13 rarely (seldom)
4 at	14 as
5 trend	15 out
6 may	16 despite (notwithstanding)
7 lead	17 authorities
8 for	18 between (among)
9 sooner	19 many
10 no	20 in

Lesson 3 Showing the Flag

C

1 What do you do (say, etc.) if (when) you see (meet, etc.) a flag seller in the street?
2 Queen Alexandra was the person (one, woman, etc.) who intro- duced Britain to the concept of selling emblems in support of charity.
3 A Danish priest gave her the idea (*or* a paraphrase – was responsi- ble for her having the idea, etc.).
4 Flags were sold for the first time on a day (*or* . . . time one day) in August 1914.
5 Societies, rather than individuals, were granted permits to collect.
6 It was said that animals caused obstruction.

D

1 There have been many radical changes (*or* Many radical changes have taken place) in the attitudes and enthusiasms which marked the birth of the British flag-day.
2 Local authorities are permitted six weeks in any one year for work of this kind (*or* this kind of work).
3 A Danish priest sold roses from his garden to help local orphans.
4 Pins were originally used to fasten the flags (*or* The flags used to be fastened with pins).
5 Adhesive emblems cost half as much as the pinned variety.
6 Adhesive emblems make hand assembly unnecessary (*or* Hand assembly is unnecessary with adhesive emblems).
7 New regulations arose from (as a result of) the rapid growth of flower and flag days.
8 The regulation probably frustrated Nell, the champion Sheffield collie.

E

1 How	11 to
2 on	12 each, every, a
3 Or	13 any
4 Whichever	14 they
5 into	15 at
6 its	16 being
7 when	17 for
8 in	18 given, sent
9 being	19 cost
10 all	20 sale

Lesson 4 Economy Drive

C

1 There has never been a better example of the philosophy of heads I win, tails you lose.
2 West Germany is the only country left in the Western World where you can drive at more than 90 mph.
3 They make no more sense today than a Victorian family house.
4 Although (some, a number of) claims have been made for them, none of them has been able to show any significant improvement in mpg figures (*or* clauses reversed).
5 The motoring magazines have not tested any that have been able to show any significant improvement in mpg figures.

D

1 With Britain's economy in such a parlous state, the motorist can't help suffering (having to suffer).
2 I think it is impossible to foresee them (for them to be foreseen) with any degree of accuracy.
3 Fuel economy will have to come first (*or* The first consideration will have to be fuel economy).
4 The graduated speed limits will probably be reduced as time goes on (*or* time clause first).
5 These levels cannot be expected if the car is not in good condition (*or* clauses reversed).
6 The kind of tune-up offered by BP makes good sense.

E

1 What
2 In
3 so
4 at
5 From
6 point
7 take
8 terms
9 one
10 where
11 at
12 say
13 over (finished) (done)
14 much
15 in
16 as
17 era (age) (epoch)
18 out
19 because
20 running (monthly, annual, etc.)

Lesson 5 Chemical Threat to Lake Nakuru

C

1 It seems certain that the life of Kenya's world famous Lake Nakuru will be destroyed (*or* It seems that the life . . . is certain to be destroyed).

2 Although there was a report which severely criticised the production procedures, Copal still has its licence (*or* Although a report appeared (was published, etc.) which . . .).

3 The report recommended that the factory should be closed immediately (*or* should immediately . . .).

4 The World Wildlife Fund suspended all new financial support (largely) because of (as a result of) the lack of government action (*or* because the government took no (did not take any) action).

5 The flamingoes were the reason why the lake area was made a national park.

6 A Netherlands university report said (stated, etc.) that a level of 0.21 mg of copper per litre would be lethal.

7 The birds use several other temporary homes, apart from Lake Nakuru (*or* The birds use several temporary homes, Lake Nakuru being one of them; *or* of which Lake Nakuru is one).

8 It is therefore doubtful whether Copal's product is competitive.

D

1 If the Copal factory goes on manufacturing copper oxychloride, the wild life will die.

2 Conservationists have been suggesting that the government should withdraw the company's permit.

3 Conservationists have been urging the government to take (away) the Company's permit away.

4 The World Wildlife Fund gave the government more than £170,000 (*or* gave more than £170,000 to the government).

5 The World Wildlife Fund is not saying (does not say) that the departure of the flamingoes is the factory's fault (the fault of the factory).

6 The effluent has not yet had time to affect the algae.

7 Once copper levels have built up they cannot be removed.

8 Once copper levels have accumulated they cannot be taken away (out).

9 What is the reason for (What reason is there for) locating the factory 400 miles from the coast?

10 Recently another factory making copper oxychloride in Nairobi did not succeed in securing an export order (recently).

E

1 it	11 instead
2 blaming (criticising, etc.)	12 were
3 from	13 make
4 yet	14 why
5 on	15 so
6 by	16 hard (difficult, etc.)
7 in	17 on
8 at	18 There
9 rest (remainder)	19 from
10 ever (good)	20 running

Lesson 6 Price of Living in the High Alps

C

1 Mountain districts come out ahead in only one respect.
2 Many people do not consider it to be an advantage that the mountain districts have more farmers.
3 The bulk of the farm work is left to their wives and children (or for their wives and children to do).
4 People usually work away from the farm in the wintertime (in or during the winter).
5 One third of the total is accounted for by mountain farms (or are mountain farms).
6 If there were no (not any) mountain farmers, the neat Swiss landscape could not be maintained.
7 Can mountain agriculture be maintained?
8 No one knows (is sure, etc.) whether it is possible to create other jobs that will not completely destroy agriculture.

D

1 They have more farmers, which many people do not think is (think of as) an advantage.
2 Seventeen per cent of the mountain population works in primary occupations, whereas only eight per cent of the total population works in them (does so). (*Work* would be acceptable in colloquial modern English).
3 They leave their wives and children to do most of the farm work (or a passive sentence – see C3 above).
4 What is the point of (anyone) resisting any extension of the mountain economy?
5 The farmers make a contribution to the food supply.
6 They stand for the Switzerland of nostalgia and holiday dreams.

E

give variety to; falling, going down; travel backwards and forwards; natural to, which are an integral part of; maintain in its natural state.

F

1 least	11 why
2 a (each) (every)	12 to
3 few	13 supply
4 half	14 own
5 as	15 must (should)
6 bulk	16 be
7 With	17 for
8 in	18 the
9 why	19 of
10 there	20 part

Lesson 7 Cost and Compassion

C

1 The reason why the arguments about helping disabled people have always been complicated is that they tend to mix up ethics and technology.
2 It has been shown that the tricycle is more unstable than four-wheelers.
3 Over 1,600 injured drivers still have claims for compensation pending (*or* paraphrase, such as 'are still waiting for their claims for compensation to be paid, settled, etc.').
4 Vehicles as safe as the four-wheeled equivalents could be supplied to people driving tricycles (*or* vehicles could be supplied . . . which would be as safe . . .).
5 This is not so much a problem of concept as of fact.
6 A mass-produced car would not only offer financial relief to the Government but might even provide a new market for the industry.

D

1 It has been government policy for many years to provide a tricycle for people (who are) capable of handling the controls.
2 The rising number of accidents caused the Government to deny that the vehicle was unsafe.
3 This decision is the one currently being reviewed (*currently* can change position).
4 Providing there are adequate funds almost any degree of handicap can be met (*or* clauses reversed).

5 The low number of drivers involved does not provide a large enough market (large enough) for mass production (*or* The market is not large enough for mass production because of the low number of drivers involved; *or* clauses reversed).

6 A conventional car with its passenger door hinged at the bottom makes the problem of access much easier for a handicapped person.

E

possessing the necessary ability, licence, permission etc.; with an engine, driven by internal combustion, etc.; practical possibility; carry it out; likely to overbalance; the amount of money provided for the purpose; does away with; growing smaller; a choice between two decisions, fulfilling neither.

F

1 tend	11 it
2 up (both)	12 best (only)
3 either (one) (any)	13 right
4 how (whether)	14 one
5 It	15 under
6 for	16 course
7 as	17 without
8 for	18 at
9 react (respond)	19 supplied (provided)
10 into	20 as

Lesson 8 Liberty v. Equality

C

1 It has always been assumed that the two aims were complementary.

2 No one has ever thought it likely that to give someone an adequate education could limit his freedom.

3 Liberty can be inhibited by (in) the application of laws designed to produce greater equality.

4 It is harder to obtain equality of opportunity if (when) there are class divisions in society.

5 It is known that the third school has a good music department.

6 What is wrong with letting parents choose the school they want their children to attend?

7 It is accepted that the school environment is of vital importance.

8 But it is the state that induces this equality of treatment.

D

1 For British reformers equality has always meant the same as equality of treatment (*or* has always been the same (thing) as equality of treatment; *or* has always meant the same treatment for everyone).
2 Central or local government can result in some loss of liberty (*or* Some loss of liberty can result from central or local government; *or* As a result of central or local government some loss of liberty can occur (be involved, etc.); *or* reversing the clauses).
3 Segregation according to ability and (segregation) on class lines are both held to be damaging (*or* Segregation, both according . . ., is held to be damaging).
4 For British reformers equality has always meant treating people the same (in the same way).
5 This is why freedom of choice that would produce inequality is prohibited (*or* This is the reason why . . .).
6 The existing town school is reputed to do good work.
7 Would liberty not be enhanced if the maximum parental choice was allowed, unless this had an adverse effect on the school system in question?
8 Would liberty not be enhanced if the maximum parental choice was allowed, provided this did not affect it adversely?

E

Inconsistent, incapable of blending; directed towards the same end; later; made more attractive or worthwhile; take it for granted; state (categorically).

F

1 to	11 would
2 was (is) (tends)	12 effect
3 make	13 reach
4 the	14 given (assuming (supposing, etc.))
5 harder	
6 if	15 room
7 does	16 another (one)
8 could (might)	17 third
9 whole (entire)	18 why
10 into	19 let
	20 attend

Lesson 9 Justice and Recompense for Victims of Crime

C

1 If you are the victim of a crime, it may not mean involvement with the formalities of criminal process.
2 The victim only enters the scene as a witness when (if) the offender has been (is) caught and charged.
3 He has little chance of receiving compensation from the offender.
4 Victims may hope for compensation from the offender.
5 Even if the offender is not convicted, assault victims may apply for a reward.
6 The judge ordered that a third of the assault victims we interviewed should get compensation (*or* ordered that compensation should be paid to a third . . . interviewed; *or* paid in a third of the cases among those we interviewed).
7 Some policemen seem to think (believe, etc.) that magistrates need encouragement.
8 Policemen suggested to victims that they might increase their chances of receiving a sum if they attended proceedings.
9 Magistrates do not always seem to take the full initiative in ordering compensation.
10 This victim was naturally dissatisfied.
11 Half of those compensated received less than the financial losses (they) (had) described.
12 It is not clear why there is this discrepancy (this discrepancy exists).

D

1 Once the offence has been reported to the police, the offender must be caught and charged.
2 A fear that it will (may) happen again?
3 Or simply to get their property back?
4 Do victims need help or advice with problems resulting from the offence?
5 Who do they turn to?
6 Assault victims may ask the Criminal Injuries Compensation Board for an award.
7 Three people attended proceedings to apply for compensation in person.
8 One or two policemen advised victims to attend proceedings because they might increase their chances of receiving a sum.
9 Sometimes the offender was caught and convicted before the victim realised how much he had suffered or spent.

E

On the spur of the moment, without premeditation; money to compensate for (make up for) injury or loss; take to court; get back; being present at; inconsistency, unfair or illogical difference.

F

1	Being	11	the
2	having	12	fear (terror)
3	must	13	Or
4	before	14	may
5	as	15	for
6	even	16	case (cases)
7	his	17	Do
8	of	18	so
9	Why	19	hands
10	report (mention)	20	them

Lesson 10 Greenwich Newly Observed

C

1 Most people who have been there think of Greenwich as (being) the Royal Naval College and the National Museum (*or* think of the Royal Naval . . . as Greenwich).

2 One project everyone is willing to applaud the GLC for is the modernization of Greenwich Pier.

3 Visitors will no longer wait in the rain for river boats.

4 The railway has never given such a good service as a 10-minute journey to London at 10-minute intervals.

5 Greenwich could be made (become) accessible without strangulation by traffic.

D

1 The attractions are likely to draw more than 10 million visitors in 1975.

2 For at least 15 years people have been saying that Greenwich was on the point of coming up (*or* had reached the point where it would come up).

3 No fewer than seven applications were submitted to the borough planning committee.

4 Attempts to bring the historic town centre back to life (give new life to the . . . centre; *or* other expressions, such as 'put new life into' . . .) will always be prejudiced.

5 A single destination board will be enough to help them find their way.

6 This pleases both Greenwich and Mr Herbert Snowball (*or* passive sentence: Both Greenwich . . . are pleased).

7 Mr Snowball counts on providing a 10-minute peak-hour frequency.

8 They could make it accessible without it (its) being strangled by traffic.

E

in large numbers; a second period of prosperity; produced, caused; changed (from one line of business to another); sort out, make a comparison in order to choose the best; how often the boats will run at the hours of the day when there are most passengers; the journey from Greenwich to Westminster, stopping at the Tower.

F

1 least	11 find
2 have	12 single
3 about (likely)	13 also
4 way	14 more
5 luck	15 tape
6 which	16 the
7 is	17 at
8 on	18 better (more)
9 No	19 ever
10 cover	20 make

Lesson 11 Walking

C

1 You swerve to one side so that he can pass (go past).

2 What is most striking about such encounters is how rarely they occur (*or* that they occur so rarely).

3 It is just as well that we are extremely good at walking.

4 If he does otherwise it is considered rude or even provocative.

5 We would rather alter our pace or even cross the road than risk having our behaviour misinterpreted.

6 We disguise our error by stopping to gaze in a shop window whose contents do not interest us.

7 Men and women appear to (apparently) adopt quite different strategies to avoid collisions.

8 Many of us will hesitate to set foot outside our front doors in case we violate the rules.

D

1 You observe that someone is coming towards you.
2 You both halt and smile apologetically at each other.
3 That we know how important it is can be gauged from the significance parents attach to a baby's first steps (*or* The significance . . . steps shows that we . . . it is).
4 Talking is the only other developmental landmark that is as eagerly awaited.
5 They filmed four hours' activity on one crossing of this kind.
6 Women turn their backs on them, however old they are and the other person is.
7 In the next few years we are likely to hear a lot more about walking.
8 We must expect psychologists and sociologists to tell us (that psychologists . . . will tell us) a lot more about walking.
9 It will sound such a complicated skill that many of us will hesitate to set foot outside our front doors.
10 This won't put off the five million Britons who think of walking as a recreation.

E

come together, come towards each other; at the same moment; both together; enormously large; make a list of; suddenly (and violently) starting; approaching; intended (likely) to cause trouble; interpreted; drawing attention to oneself in a showy way.

F

1 as	11 breaking
2 how	12 holding
3 without (lacking)	13 each
4 how	14 most
5 Who	15 turned (reached)
6 walker (pedestrian)	16 with
7 do	17 make
8 too	18 together
9 up	19 on
10 allow	20 at

Lesson 12 The Sun Sinks Slowly on the Western

C

1 Making a western was the solution to the financial woes caused by too many flops.
2 No film of John Wayne's ever lost money, and most westerns were quite profitable whether the Duke was in them or not.
3 The networks not only created their own westerns but also bought the longer Hollywood versions (*or* The networks created their . . . and also bought . . .).
4 Those few are neither very good nor particularly successful.
5 It seems that the old slipper has burst at the seams.
6 Police and detective series have (virtually) replaced Westerns on (*or*, which have virtually disappeared from) prime-time television.
7 The crucial factors are not the interests of producers and audience but (as much as) those of technique (*or* The crucial factors are not so much the interests . . . as those . . .).
8 The merit of this approach is that it makes the explanation take into account the social context of the film.

D

1 (For years) Cowboys and Indians used to be the staples of the screen.
2 Hollywood has owed its continued popularity and success to the Western.
3 Hollywood's continued popularity and success have been due to the Western.
4 Understandably the genre attracts film-makers much less.
5 This assumes that the crucial factors are technical ones.
6 We can see only what they let us see.
7 Each of these explanations probably has some validity.
8 The audience takes an active part.

E

1 In (During)	11 lack
2 Few	12 one
3 or	13 As
4 seems (appears)	14 longer
5 so (it)	15 makes
6 without (lacking)	16 less
7 their	17 lose
8 just	18 in
9 like	19 from
10 unlike	20 to

Section Three: Progress Tests

Test 1

Selective Cloze Test

1 kind, sort (type)	11 one
2 likely (going)	12 rising, growing, increasing
3 ask	13 keeping
4 like	14 so
5 whatever	15 shortage, crisis
6 taste, nourishment (good)	16 sufficiently, very
7 course	17 those
8 why	18 even
9 future	19 in
10 hand	20 ourselves

Dialogue 1

1 can I do
2 was (just) going to
3 isn't it
4 would never (wouldn't) know
5 get used
6 moved (came) into
7 want to, intend to
8 telling
9 cut, lower
10 rid of

Dialogue 2

1 you seen
2 goes
3 's going on
4 must have gone, may
   have gone, has
   probably gone
5 he is, he comes
6 will you, are you going to
7 are getting
8 takes
9 were going, could go
10 'll, 'll be able to

Structural Conversion 1

1 I was so tired that I couldn't walk any further.
2 As I felt too tired to walk any further, I took a taxi.
3 Neither of us knew where John was.
4 Neither her father nor I saw her yesterday.
5 Both of them are worth reading.
6 She must have missed her train.
7 Did he explain why he behaved like that?
8 There's no reason for you to come (you coming) (your coming) if you don't want to.
9 In spite of the rain (of the fact that it was raining), they went on playing.
10 Even if they offer him more money, it won't make any difference.
11 You were bored to death with the play before the end, like (and so was) everyone else.

12 He's likely to turn up late.

13 We're likely to have good weather for our trip.

14 I hardly ever watch that programme.

15 My wife is going to leave my dinner on the stove, in case she has to go out.

16 I'm in no hurry. Herbert is the one who's pressing for a decision.

17 She'll never forgive him, whatever he says.

18 We didn't get a ticket in the end, in spite of queuing (having queued) up for three hours.

19 Susan hasn't written to (been in touch with) me recently.

20 I've got enough problems of my own, without having to cope (coping) with yours as well.

Structural Conversion 2

1 I don't think he's capable of doing the job.

2 You shouldn't take any notice of what she says.

3 I convinced him that he should go with me.

4 I insist on knowing the truth.

5 It would be typical of him to do a thing like that.

6 He's obviously interested in promotion.

7 We're likely to have a spell of bad weather.

8 We've run out of milk, I'm afraid.

9 What time are they showing the game on television this evening?

10 Only George didn't like the show (*or* George was the only one who didn't like the show).

11 Did he give a (any) reason why he was late (for being late)?

12 He hasn't paid back the money he borrowed from me.

13 He doesn't like being by himself.

14 He wasn't well enough to make the journey.

15 What time does the plane arrive in New York?

16 He's lived here all his life.

17 I'll put you up for the night, if you've nowhere to stay.

18 I'm surprised he turned down your offer.

19 She looks down on us because she went to such an expensive school.

20 I'll stand by the agreement, whatever the rest of them do.

Test 2

Selective Cloze Test 1

1 there
2 place
3 in
4 glancing, looking
5 newspaper(s)
6 same
7 explaining
8 copies
9 worth
10 at

11 being
12 between
13 claim, try, attempt
14 to
15 at
16 birth
17 every
18 on
19 forecast, newspaper
20 tells

Selective Cloze Test 2

1 course
2 for
3 their
4 even
5 make
6 use, good
7 take, get
8 across
9 without
10 words, things

11 glance
12 for
13 rather
14 unless
15 whole, entire, complete
16 ago
17 much (fast) (slowly)
18 how
19 instead
20 well

Dialogue

1 was no one (nobody)
2 came, turned up, arrived
3 had never seen (met)
4 What was he like?
5 to talk to, to chat up

6 talking
7 make matters (things)
8 would have happened
9 Are you going to, Will you, Are you likely to
10 will be back, is going to be back

Structural Conversion 1

1 Since he was a teacher himself, he was able to understand the problem involved.
2 A cousin of mine is spending the weekend with us.
3 There was no one for him to talk to.
4 He has a lot of people working under him.
5 We would have crashed if I hadn't braked.
6 I wouldn't have had all this trouble if you'd told me earlier.
7 It's the first time I've (ever) been here.

8 Why does he want to borrow your car? He's got a car of his own.

9 There's no reason why he should complain.

10 Such famous film stars as Elizabeth Taylor and Richard Burton attended the première.

11 Their English is certain to improve in time.

12 I suggested that he should try to cut down his smoking.

13 The Prime Minister is believed to be planning to resign.

14 He is said to take after me.

15 A number of other people are thought to have been involved in the affair.

16 It is dangerous to cross the railway lines to get to the beach.

17 Falling in love is a wonderful experience.

18 One never knows what's going to happen, does one?

19 It was unfair of him to blame me for his mistakes.

20 You had better do it again.

Structural Conversion 2

1 He explained it all to me (*or* everything that had happened to me).

2 To tell the truth, I don't understand what you mean.

3 We hardly ever get inquiries of that kind.

4 Of course it belongs to me.

5 It's just like him to turn up half an hour late.

6 There's no point in arguing about it.

7 She's a pleasure (*or* very pleasant) to talk to.

8 You can't rely on him to carry out instructions.

9 Since there was no further business, the meeting broke up at 10 o'clock.

10 He ought to get on with his own work, rather than interfere with everyone else.

11 Did you succeed in reaching an agreement?

12 It turned out to be more difficult than he had expected.

13 I'd rather have tea, if you don't mind.

14 I object to working overtime unless I'm paid for it.

15 The noise almost drove me mad.

16 I don't approve of the way they bring up their children.

17 You need not have tried to persuade me. I'd have done it of my own accord.

18 How do you account for the difference between his story and yours?

19 I'll look into your complaint, Madam, and find out who was responsible.

20 What happened wasn't my fault.

Test 3

Selective Cloze Test 1

1 Even	11 in
2 on	12 one
3 similar	13 thousands (hundreds)
4 far (much)	14 make
5 cope (deal)	15 since
6 where	16 level
7 so	17 which
8 shares	18 case (event)
9 being	19 looking
10 be	20 light

Selective Cloze Test 2

1 come	11 more
2 read	12 above
3 which	13 no
4 much	14 majority
5 one (that)	15 place
6 taking (gaining) (getting)	16 which
7 whether	17 capable
8 used	18 in
9 ground(s)	19 more (but) (yet)
10 was	20 whose

Dialogue 1

1 how (where) you got (what gave you)	6 must have asked
2 know (find out about, etc.)	7 would happen to
3 don't mind (don't object to)	8 asking
4 must be aware	9 should have, ought to have
5 had occurred, has occurred	10 am

Dialogue 2

1 was talking, speaking	6 am writing, have to write, want to write
2 been interested, been involved, specialised	7 has anything to do, has something to do, is connected
3 was talking, speaking *or* spoke *or* mentioned it	8 looking at, seeing
4 might be, would be	9 will be, are going to be
5 am doing *or* am interested in, etc.	10 what he looked like

Structural Conversion 1

1 His idea is not as (so) sensible as yours.
2 Her sister is not nearly as (so) likely to win as she is (*or* is far less likely . . .).
3 His honesty, more than anything else, is what I like about him.
4 Their problems are similar to ours (*or* Their problems and ours are similar).
5 Do you think we are alike?
6 Five years ago, the situation was not the same (as it is now).
7 I don't know what gave you the idea I'm rich.
8 I agree that we haven't done as much as we could to help.
9 The closure of the school was a blow to the teachers, many of whom had worked there for years.
10 Sitting around waiting is not as good as keeping busy.
11 The older I get, the more irritable I become.
12 I am very interested in antiques, but what interests me most (above all) is silverware.
13 It's very kind of you to say such things.
14 I can't explain why he behaved like that (*or* his behaving like that).
15 They have been accustomed to disasters of this kind for a long time.
16 I'm afraid I'm going to (I will) disappoint you.
17 I won't take up much of your time.
18 He isn't very fond of (keen on) apples.
19 I've never met such a rude man.
20 You'd still have lost, however well you'd played.

Structural Conversion 2

1 He's bound to know the answer.
2 A brilliant plan suddenly occurred to him.
3 Her characters remind me of those of Graham Greene.
4 The Company decided to drop out of the battle.
5 I was surprised that he was capable of doing it.
6 The difference between us is that I have a family to support.
7 Who recommended me to you?
8 Who put you on to me?
9 It was built just over fifty years ago.
10 I've never understood how they are (were) connected.
11 We were all there, apart from John.
12 The only thing he cares about is money.
13 I hope you don't object to me (my) saying this.
14 There is a risk of fire(s) breaking out at any time.
15 Superintendent Jones is in charge of (heading) the inquiry into the crime.

16 I'm told we are liable to have good weather at that time of year.
17 Is that the man you were in conversation with (having a conversation with) just now?
18 I think it's preferable to go out to work rather than (and not) stay at home all day (*or* instead of staying . . .).
19 He's an awful man. I don't know how she can put up with him.
20 She has got over her illness.

Test 4

Selective Cloze Test

1	of	11	come
2	such	12	asking
3	whom	13	in
4	doing	14	aware
5	under	15	make
6	one (that)	16	wearing (in)
7	how	17	in
8	were	18	Only
9	order	19	whether
10	much (far)	20	managed

Dialogue

1 make yourself*
2 will depend (depends)
3 to get to know (meet)
4 to ask
5 don't take it
6 what (anything) you say
7 won't be held (used)
8 Have you always been interested
9 runs
10 (must) take after

*Some paraphrases are possible – 'behave as if you were', for example – though they do not sound so natural.

Structural Conversion 1

1 It was clear to everyone that he had been the man responsible for the crime.
2 The problem that concerns us is why (that) he didn't admit it.
3 The policeman asked what he had been doing the night before.
4 She asked me if I knew whether (if) the race had finished (yet).
5 She asked me not to do it again.
6 I advised her to go to the reception desk.
7 She complained that I hadn't helped her as much as I should have done.
8 She offered to go with me (if I liked).

9 It's such a pleasant surprise to meet you again!
10 I'll always remember how good he was to me.
11 I'll never forget what a terrible state she was in.
12 He raised his hand and, in doing so, knocked the lamp over.
13 He's getting too absent-minded to go on working any longer.
14 Everyone (who was) present was in agreement with the proposal.
15 This is the procedure that every student has to follow.
16 There are two additional papers but neither of them is compulsory.
17 Whether he should go or not is for him to decide (*or* his decision; *or* up to him, etc.).
18 They shouldn't let people like that join the club.
19 You had better leave now, before the rain starts.
20 It's time you made up your mind.

Structural Conversion 2

1 Who is in charge of this department?
2 I'm not afraid of the consequences (*or* The consequences don't make me afraid).
3 How did he reply to the accusations?
4 What attracts me to (about) this method is that it's simple.
5 He refused to stand up.
6 I accused him of stealing it.
7 She apologised for being (arriving) late.
8 He suggested that we should pool (we pooled) our ideas.
9 Don't take it to heart.
10 There's no need to make such a fuss about it.
11 The results of our research cannot be put into effect immediately.
12 It's going to cost rather a lot (*or* The cost (of it) is going to be rather high).
13 We're not prepared to commit ourselves at this moment.
14 Have you always been interested in becoming a doctor?
15 He made a joke.
16 He had his tongue in his cheek.
17 They are out of date.
18 He was afraid that his fingerprints would give him away.
19 I'm afraid they're out of stock (*or* we haven't any in stock).
20 I convinced him in the end (*or* In the end, I . . .).

Test 5

Selective Cloze Test

1 answering	11 fault
2 First	12 to
3 makes (made)	13 get
4 up	14 in
5 for	15 of
6 as	16 sense (reason)
7 For	17 as
8 playing	18 than
9 deal	19 had
10 place	20 done

Dialogue

1 me (my) interrupting, bothering, etc.	6 have finished
2 Could	7 haven't been
3 better deal (better get on)	8 can make (make)
4 Let's	9 Let's get (Get) (Come)
5 see you (speak to you, etc.)	10 there is (I've got)

Structural Conversion 1

1 I'd rather you signed the cheque now.
2 He may not have realised what he had to do at first.
3 I finally succeeded in convincing him of its value.
4 He works for an engineering firm, like us.
5 Such famous players as Cruyff and Luis Pereira took part in the game.
6 Would you mind explaining it to me again, please?
7 He may not have been working here long but he's already impressed the manager.
8 I asked her if I could help her.
9 The manager said that there might be a logical explanation, but he couldn't think of one.
10 Keith told Mr Bristow that he had reason to believe that someone might have been embezzling the firm's money.
11 Should she feel worse during the night, give her these tablets.
12 Were the painting to prove valuable, it would be a pity to have given it away.
13 Had we been consulted, we could have given you good advice.
14 We'll end the meeting here, provided you have no further questions.
15 I wish it weren't (wasn't) such a long way.

16 If only he hadn't missed it.
17 Would you like me to get the tickets for you?
18 Let's not argue about it.
19 If you had Mr Bramley for a boss, you'd know what hard work's like.
20 I must get my suit cleaned.

Structural Conversion 2

1 I've no objection to paying for it.
2 I think you've made a mistake.
3 I can hardly believe it (*or* It's hardly possible for me . . .).
4 He advised me to take this medicine.
5 Would you like me to go through (over) them for you?
6 We can't rule out candidates because of their political opinions (*or* rule candidates out . . .).
7 He has applied for the job (in writing).
8 From now on, you will be in charge of the factory.
9 It looks (like) a wonderful opportunity (*or* It looks as if it would be (is) a wonderful opportunity).
10 The committee have put off their decision until the next meeting.
11 Your health will stand up to it, provided you don't try to do too much.
12 I never expected him to turn down our offer.
13 An appointment must be made immediately (*or* We (they, etc.) must make an appointment immediately).
14 Things are always going wrong in a job of this sort (*or* this sort of job).
15 She's got enough on her hands, without helping you with your work.
16 He might turn out (to be) worse than the present manager once you got to know him.
17 He needn't have lost his temper.
18 He bought her a present to make up for being rude to her.
19 I can't stand working for him. He gets on my nerves.
20 He said he was fed up with listening to my complaints.

Test 6

Selective Cloze Test

1	in	11	who
2	any	12	had
3	so	13	at
4	spite	14	could
5	deal	15	his
6	more	16	on
7	Although (Though)	17	than
8	for	18	in
9	as	19	which
10	as	20	in

Dialogue

1	are having, are going to have	6	used to
2	haven't eaten	7	It's
3	went out	8	have married
4	to be	9	Haven't
5	rather (sooner) have	10	let me

Structural Conversion 1

 1 He wasn't allowed to play with other children.
 2 She hasn't written to me for ages.
 3 It's the first time I've ever seen anything like that.
 4 He's such a strong man that he can pick up two men at once.
 5 He came in quietly so as not to wake up his wife.
 6 He hadn't anything (had nothing) to do.
 7 She's tall but her father's taller still (than she is) (than her).
 8 He preferred to come by bus, rather than take a taxi.
 9 It has already been paid for.
10 At the time when he was born, the system of government was being changed.
11 He must have been thought of as an important man to have been given such treatment.
12 Fred suggested that we (they) should go (that we (they) went).
13 They didn't let her go out.
14 She insured her life, in case she had an accident.
15 Never could he have imagined that he would become famous.
16 Under no circumstances will I ever consent to it.
17 Only when there was no hope of victory did they surrender.
18 They both worked hard but Sheila was the only one to pass (that passed) (who passed) the examination.

19 She won't do it, and neither will I.
20 He won a prize and so did his sister.

Structural Conversion 2

1 I don't see anything to complain about (of) in the new regulations.
2 I was on the point of doing it myself.
3 I'm afraid they've been held up by the heavy traffic.
4 (As I was) On my (the) way to the station, I met Margaret.
5 He asked her to marry him.
6 Haven't you made up your mind yet?
7 He insisted on coming with me (or He insisted that he would come with me) whether I liked it or not.
8 It's never occurred to me before.
9 It was a great pleasure (It gave him great pleasure) to see (He took great pleasure in seeing) so many old friends again.
10 He is considered to be the greatest actor in the world.
11 It would be worth (while) looking at (it).
12 His education had an influence on (over) him for the rest of his life.
13 The captain did not want to put the lives of his crew in danger.
14 We have given him the name of Alexander.
15 He had to retire because of his age.
16 He's quite an easy-going man.
17 He's tall, but his father's even taller.
18 The agent described it as a magnificent, modern house (or The agent described the house as magnificent and modern).
19 It doesn't appeal to me very much.
20 He's short of money.

Section Four: Test Papers

Test Paper 1 – Section A

1

1 being	11 like
2 made	12 whom
3 of	13 as
4 side	14 wheel
5 In	15 whose
6 still	16 suffered
7 involved	17 second (other)
8 before	18 lose
9 drive	19 such
10 leads	20 in

2

1 The box was too heavy for him to lift.
2 Neither my brother nor I learnt much at school.
3 In spite of the fine weather (the weather being fine), they decided to stay indoors.
4 I wasn't worried about it. Jack was the one who got upset.
5 They are a pleasure to talk to (pleasant to talk to).
6 One never knows where one is with people like that, does one?
7 I agree that we didn't make as (so) good a job of it as we could have done.
8 She begged me not to blame her for it.
9 I wish it weren't (wasn't) too late to do anything about it.
10 Not until early the following year was he able to take up the post.

3

1 says*	6 don't you look
2 get back, return, etc.	7 should have finished (done)
3 him to do	8 will have done
4 could have gone	9 have been
5 you did	10 what it is (was) like, how frightening it is (was)

*'is saying' or 'has said' possible in some contexts.

4

1 Did he give any reason for behaving like that (for such
behaviour)?
2 I'm afraid I don't agree with you.
3 His father did not approve of what he had done.
4 The evidence shows that he told the truth.
5 There's no point in losing your temper.
6 His speech went down well with the audience.
7 You shouldn't take any notice of what he says.
8 I hope you don't object to me (my) talking to you like this.
9 They've given her a rise in salary (*or* (less common) a salary rise).
10 I'm going to put you in charge of the afternoon shift.

Test Paper 2 – Section A

1

1 their	11 what
2 no	12 getting
3 have (get)	13 another
4 listening	14 in
5 which	15 most (only)
6 on	16 got
7 in	17 if
8 front	18 why
9 audience	19 anything
10 or	20 say

2

1 He's said to be getting married next month.
2 It's the first time I've ever seen a man with six fingers.
3 His opponent is not nearly as (so) likely (*or* far less likely) to be
elected than he is (him).
4 It was obvious to everyone that he was the guilty man.
5 I'll never forget how kind they were to me.
6 He apologised for being so rude to me (her, etc).
7 We had better call the fire brigade, before the fire spreads.
8 Let's not quarrel.
9 Would you mind repeating the question (please)?
10 I've written her a note, in case she forgets.

3

1 have been working	6 wouldn't . . .*
2 are operating (working, etc.)	7 was (just) going to ring**
3 would (might) have got wet	8 could have kept (remained)
4 will be able to	9 should (ought to) have
5 make you	heard
	10 what (who) you're talking

*almost any 'irritating' verb will do – whistle, sing, hum, etc.
**or was about to ring, was on the point of ringing.

4

1 He's obviously interested in making his fortune.
2 I insist on knowing what happened.
3 When their parents died, an aunt of theirs brought them up.
4 She had a blue dress on.
5 You shouldn't let them take advantage of you.
6 It doesn't matter to me whether we go or not.
7 I'd rather have coffee, if it's all the same to you.
8 It's not my fault.
9 He is considered to be the world's leading authority on the subject.
10 The difference between us is that I'm due to retire next year.

Test Paper 3 – Section A

1

1 what	11 top
2 other	12 deal (cope)
3 lays	13 rid
4 act	14 mistake
5 those	15 belongs
6 one	16 how
7 making	17 takes
8 as	18 brought
9 place	19 most
10 nest	20 few

2

1 She hasn't written to me recently.
2 He is believed to have had a number of accomplices.
3 It was unkind of him to say it was my fault.
4 The more I see of him, the less I like him.
5 I won't take up much of your time.
6 I've never met such an intelligent (a more intelligent) man.

7 Whether he accepts the appointment or not is up to him to decide.
8 He spoke softly so as not to wake the baby.
9 I must get my trousers cleaned.
10 We'll stop now, provided you haven't any (have no) further questions.

3

1 have been looking for
2 have been in for, entered for, etc.
3 hadn't spoken
4 couldn't have done
5 Let's go

6 have never seen, heard of, etc.
7 been brought up
8 he likes it or not, you approve or not, etc.
9 was I to know, was I expected to know
10 have kept you

4

1 He's lived here all his life.
2 Nylon clothes catch fire very easily.
3 Hang on to the rail! You might fall off the bus.
4 He was given the sack for being incompetent.
5 Did you succeed in finishing the job?
6 I didn't think he would be capable of doing it.
7 I take it for granted that you'll be at the meeting tonight.
8 He applied (to me) for a job.
9 The new plan cannot be put into effect immediately.
10 He's quite a tall fellow.

Test Paper 4 – Section A

1

1 such
2 an (any)
3 opposite (contrary)
4 to
5 that
6 speaking
7 as
8 own
9 as
10 which

11 taking
12 both
13 whether
14 place
15 According
16 as
17 so
18 able
19 like
20 do

2

1 He's likely to be late.
2 I'd have killed the cat if I hadn't seen it.
3 Learning to speak another language fluently is not easy.
4 You were tired, like everyone else (all the rest of us).
5 I like Dutch painting, but what I like most are Rembrandt's portraits.
6 She asked him where he had been when she rang (had rung) him.
7 She said there might be a good reason for it but she couldn't imagine what it was.
8 Would you like me to come with you?
9 At that time, agricultural workers were being driven into the cities by (the) low wages.
10 He must have been highly thought of to have been given the job (*or* for them to have given him the job).

3

1 gets
2 to have caught, jumped on, etc.
3 was able to, managed to
4 had taken your
5 needn't have done

6 have stayed
7 had taken place, occurred, etc.
8 have (already) spoken
9 have made you
10 to report, to go, etc.

4

1 I can hardly understand it.
2 I'm used to getting up early, so I don't find it a hardship.
3 Things are always going wrong in a school of this kind (this kind of school).
4 I'm not afraid of anything (afraid of nothing).
5 I made it clear to him that I wouldn't accept any more excuses.
6 The weather was fine when we set out for London.
7 The court found him not guilty on all counts.
8 He was not well enough to go with them.
9 Such famous conductors as Toscanini and Beecham have conducted here (*or* Famous conductors such as Toscanini . . .).
10 They described it as the best performance they had ever seen.

Structural Conversion Index

The lessons referred to are those in *Proficiency English Book 1*, where structural conversions are practised.